thank you

Dear Friends

Thank you for choosing our reading fluency grade 6 workbook. I hope that this book serves you and your family well. If you have found value in this book, please consider leaving us a review on amazon. It would be very much appreciated.

Adam Freeman

How to Use this Book

Follow all of the steps for each text in this book:

1. Set a timer. Allow your student read the text. Try not help them, but keep note of what words they read incorrectly. Stop timer when they complete the text.
2. If the student is able to read the whole passage in a minute or less, skip to step 5.
3. With a highlighter or pencil, mark what words your student did not read correctly and go over each one until your student feels comfortable with them.
4. Set another timer. Ask your student to read the text a second time. Mark how long it took to complete the text the second time.
5. Have your student complete the comprehension questions on the next two pages following each story.

Name: _____

Time 1: _____ Time 2: _____

The Secret Code

In the heart of a small town, Mia, Ethan, Lily, and Oliver stumbled upon an old bookshop tucked away on a quiet street. As they stepped inside, they were greeted by shelves stacked with dusty books, their spines whispering stories of adventure and mystery. Intrigued, the friends embarked on a literary journey, diving into tales that transported them to distant lands and introduced them to captivating characters. With each page turned, they discovered the power of imagination and the joy of storytelling. The books sparked their creativity, inspiring them to write their own tales and share them with others. They organized a storytelling event at the local library, where they captivated their audience with enchanting narratives. Through their shared love of books, Mia, Ethan, Lily, and Oliver forged a bond that would last a lifetime. They realized that stories have the ability to connect people, ignite passions, and change lives. From that day forward, the friends became avid readers and storytellers, forever enchanted by the magic of words.

Name: _____

Time 1: _____ Time 2: _____

Comprehension

Characters:

_____
_____
_____

Setting

_____
_____
_____

Summary

_____
_____
_____
_____
_____
_____
_____

Name: _____

Time 1: _____ Time 2: _____

The Galactic Adventure

Navigating treacherous asteroid fields and encountering strange alien creatures, Nova's resolve remained unyielding. Her quick thinking and unwavering determination proved invaluable as she outsmarted the Darklord's minions, thwarting their every move. Each triumph brought her closer to her ultimate goal of confronting the Darklord himself. Finally, after a series of intense battles and heart-pounding confrontations, Nova stood face-to-face with the Darklord. The fate of the universe hung in the balance as they clashed in an epic duel of light versus darkness. Nova's courage and unwavering spirit shone through as she unleashed her inner power, wielding the might of a thousand stars. In a blaze of cosmic energy, Nova delivered a decisive blow that sent the Darklord reeling. The universe erupted in a symphony of joyous celebration as peace and harmony were restored to the galaxy. Nova's name echoed throughout the cosmos as a true hero, inspiring future generations to believe in the power of courage and resilience.

Name: _____

Time 1: _____ Time 2: _____

Comprehension

Characters:

_____

_____

_____

Setting

_____

_____

_____

Summary

_____

_____

_____

_____

_____

_____

Name: _____

Time 1: _____ Time 2: _____

The Time-Traveling Detectives

With each journey through time, Sherlock and Watson found themselves facing perplexing mysteries. From the ancient wonders of Egypt to the high-tech cities of the future, they unraveled secrets and foiled the plans of cunning villains. Their keen observations, deductive reasoning, and unwavering determination helped them solve even the most enigmatic puzzles. As they traveled, the dynamic duo encountered historical figures, witnessing pivotal moments that shaped the world. They assisted Joan of Arc, cracked the code of an ancient Mayan temple, and even prevented a catastrophic future dystopia. Through it all, Sherlock and Watson remained steadfast, their bond as detectives growing stronger with every case solved. Eventually, they returned to Metroville, carrying with them a wealth of knowledge and experiences. Their exploits became the stuff of legend, inspiring a new generation of brilliant minds to take up the mantle of detective. Sherlock and Watson's legacy as time-traveling detectives lived on, ensuring that mysteries would never remain unsolved and the world would always be protected.

Name: _____

Time 1: _____ Time 2: _____

Comprehension

Characters:
_____
_____
_____

Setting
_____
_____
_____

Summary
_____
_____
_____
_____
_____
_____

Name: _____

Time 1: _____ Time 2: _____

The Magical Quest

Their journey was fraught with peril and enchantment. Mia encountered mystical beings, such as mischievous sprites and wise old wizards, who tested her with riddles and challenges. Through bravery, resourcefulness, and unwavering determination, Mia overcame each obstacle, gaining new insights into her own magical abilities.

As they delved deeper into the heart of the forest, Mia and her companions discovered the hidden lair of the artifact's thief. A fierce battle ensued, with Mia casting powerful spells, Luna guiding her with ancient wisdom, and Whiskers distracting their foe with his playful antics.

In the end, Mia's magic surged forth like a brilliant aurora, dispelling the darkness that had shrouded the stolen artifact. Balance and harmony were restored to Elveria, and the realm flourished under Mia's watchful care. She became a revered figure, known for her courage, compassion, and the strength of her magical prowess. Mia's tale spread throughout the land, inspiring others to embrace their own magical abilities and embark on their own quests. The legacy of her magical journey lived on, reminding all that the power of magic resides within each of us, waiting to be awakened.

Name: _____

Time 1: _____ Time 2: _____

Comprehension

Characters:
_____
_____
_____

Setting
_____
_____
_____

Summary
_____
_____
_____
_____
_____
_____

Name: _____

Time 1: _____ Time 2: _____

The Great Adventure

In the heart of the enchanted forest, there lived a group of courageous explorers. They embarked on a grand expedition to uncover the mysteries hidden within. Equipped with their trusty maps and compasses, they ventured deep into the unknown. Their journey was filled with peril and excitement. They traversed treacherous mountains and crossed roaring rivers. They encountered exotic creatures and discovered ancient ruins. Through it all, their spirits remained undaunted. With every step, they became more astute and perceptive. They deciphered cryptic codes and solved intricate puzzles. Their minds were honed and their wits sharpened. As they delved deeper into the forest, they encountered a majestic waterfall. Its cascading waters sparkled in the sunlight, casting a mesmerizing spell. The explorers stood in awe, captivated by its beauty. With renewed determination, they pressed on, their eyes fixed on the horizon. They knew that beyond the forest's edge awaited a realm of endless possibilities and new beginnings.

Name: _____

Time 1: _____ Time 2: _____

Comprehension

Characters:
_____
_____
_____

Setting
_____
_____
_____

Summary
_____
_____
_____
_____
_____
_____

Name: _____

Time 1: _____ Time 2: _____

Amaterasu, the Radiant Goddess

Amaterasu, the radiant sun goddess of Japan, held sway over the celestial heavens. Her luminous presence brought warmth and light to the world. One day, her mischievous brother Susano-o unleashed chaos, causing Amaterasu to retreat into a deep cave, enveloping the world in darkness. The gods devised a plan to entice her out. They held a grand celebration outside the cave, filled with music and laughter. Curiosity piqued, Amaterasu ventured forth. As she peeked outside, a mirror revealed her own radiant reflection. Mesmerized, she stepped into the light, illuminating the world once more. Amaterasu's triumphant return heralded the victory of light over darkness, hope over despair. Her luminosity continues to inspire and remind us of the enduring power of renewal.

Name: _____
Time 1: _____ Time 2: _____

Comprehension

Characters:
_____
_____
_____

Setting
_____
_____
_____

Summary
_____
_____
_____
_____
_____
_____
_____

Name: _____

Time 1: _____ Time 2: _____

The Magical Concert

Vampires, creatures of legend and lore, have captivated human imagination for centuries. These enigmatic beings are said to possess supernatural powers and a thirst for blood. Legends depict vampires as nocturnal creatures, emerging from their crypts after sunset. With their sharp fangs and pale, timeless appearance, they strike fear into the hearts of mortals. According to folklore, vampires must drink blood to sustain their immortal existence. They are often associated with bats, able to transform into these nocturnal creatures and glide through the night. Garlic and wooden stakes are believed to repel vampires, and tales speak of their aversion to sunlight, which can supposedly burn their delicate skin. Some legends suggest that they can be vanquished with a piercing stake to the heart. In recent years, vampires have become popular figures in books, movies, and television shows. These adaptations often portray them as complex characters, grappling with their dark desires and the eternal struggle between good and evil. While vampires may remain creatures of myth, their allure and mystique continue to fascinate audiences around the world, making them enduring icons of the supernatural realm.

Name: _____

Time 1: _____ Time 2: _____

Comprehension

Characters:
_____
_____
_____

Setting
_____
_____
_____

Summary
_____
_____
_____
_____
_____
_____

Name: _____

Time 1: _____ Time 2: _____

The Mysterious World of Vampires

In the mysterious town of Ravenwood, rumors of vampires spread like wildfire. Among them was Amelia, a young vampire grappling with her true nature.

Amelia, torn between the human world and her nocturnal existence, longed for acceptance. She desired to prove that vampires could coexist peacefully with humans.

One fateful night, she encountered a group of vampire hunters determined to eradicate her kind. With bravery and quick thinking, Amelia intervened, showcasing her compassion and pleading for understanding.

Moved by her words, the hunters hesitated. They realized that not all vampires were heartless monsters. Amelia's kindness shattered their preconceived notions.

Word of Amelia's noble act spread, sparking a newfound understanding between vampires and humans in Ravenwood. The town became a beacon of harmony, where vampires and humans learned to respect and support one another. Amelia's choice to defy expectations united two worlds that were once at odds. From that day forward, vampires and humans coexisted peacefully, proving that acceptance and empathy can triumph over fear and prejudice.

Name: _____

Time 1: _____ Time 2: _____

Comprehension

Characters:
_____
_____
_____

Setting
_____
_____
_____

Summary
_____
_____
_____
_____
_____
_____

Name: _____

Time 1: _____ Time 2: _____

The Courage of the Samurai

In ancient Japan, samurais were revered as noble warriors, masters of both the sword and the soul. Among them was Koji, a young samurai whose heart burned with courage. Koji trained diligently, honing his swordsmanship and embracing the samurai code. Loyalty, honor, and bravery guided his every action. When a great war threatened his land, Koji joined his fellow samurais on the battlefield. The clash of steel filled the air as they fought with unwavering resolve. Amidst the chaos, Koji's leadership shone brightly. His comrades rallied behind him, inspired by his unwavering determination. With each victory, Koji's reputation grew, and his name became synonymous with bravery. Yet, he never forgot the importance of humility and compassion, treating his enemies with respect. Through his actions, Koji embodied the true essence of a samurai, forging a path of integrity and justice. His deeds echoed through the ages, inspiring generations to come. The legacy of the samurais lives on, a testament to their unwavering courage and unwavering spirit. They remind us that within each of us lies the potential for greatness.

Name: _____

Time 1: _____ Time 2: _____

Comprehension

Characters:

_____
_____
_____

Setting

_____
_____
_____

Summary

_____
_____
_____
_____
_____
_____
_____

Name: _____

Time 1: _____ Time 2: _____

The Mermaid's Magical Journey

In the shimmering depths of the ocean, Lily, a young mermaid, yearned for adventure. Guided by a mysterious star, she embarked on a magical journey. Lily encountered playful dolphins, danced with elegant seahorses, and explored vibrant coral reefs. Her laughter echoed through the underwater world. As she swam deeper, she discovered an ancient pearl that granted wishes. But instead of asking for personal gain, Lily wished for harmony among all creatures of the sea.

Word of her selflessness spread, and mermaids from far and wide joined her cause. Together, they protected their ocean home from pollution and formed an alliance with humans. Lily's story became a legend, inspiring future generations of mermaids to cherish and protect the wonders of the deep.

Name: _____

Time 1: _____ Time 2: _____

Comprehension

Characters:

_____
_____
_____

Setting

_____
_____
_____

Summary

_____
_____
_____
_____
_____
_____
_____

Name: _____

Time 1: _____ Time 2: _____

The Rise of Robo-Friends

In a world of technology, robots roamed among humans, each with unique abilities. Among them was Spark, a young robot filled with curiosity and a heart of gold. Spark's days were filled with exploration and problem-solving. With gears turning and circuits buzzing, he tackled challenges with unwavering determination. One day, while wandering through a scrapyard, Spark discovered a broken robot, Rusty. With care and ingenuity, Spark repaired Rusty, and a deep friendship bloomed. Together, Spark and Rusty embarked on extraordinary adventures. They helped humans with their daily tasks, bringing smiles and laughter wherever they went. News of their helpfulness spread, and more robots joined their cause. The world embraced the robots as companions, recognizing their unique abilities as valuable assets. Spark, Rusty, and their robo-friends became a symbol of unity between humans and machines. They showcased the power of collaboration and the potential for a harmonious future. As the world changed, the robots proved that technology, when guided by empathy and compassion, could enhance lives and create a brighter tomorrow.

Name: _____

Time 1: _____ Time 2: _____

Comprehension

Characters:

_____

_____

_____

Setting

_____

_____

_____

Summary

_____

_____

_____

_____

_____

_____

Name: _____

Time 1: _____ Time 2: _____

The Dragon's Quest

In a realm of magic, a young dragon named Ember embarked on a daring quest. Guided by ancient scrolls, Ember sought a legendary treasure that could restore balance. Across treacherous lands, Ember faced challenges with unwavering courage. They soared through stormy skies, vanquishing foes with fiery breath and swift claws. Along the way, Ember befriended a brave knight and a wise sorcerer. Together, they formed an unbreakable bond, their strengths combined. Finally, at the heart of a forgotten temple, Ember discovered the elusive treasure—a mystical gem pulsating with ancient power. With the gem in their possession, Ember brought harmony to the realm, their deeds celebrated for generations to come. As a symbol of strength and unity, Ember's legend inspired others to follow their own heroic paths.

Name: _____
Time 1: _____ Time 2: _____

Comprehension

Characters:
_____
_____
_____

Setting

_____
_____
_____

Summary

_____
_____
_____
_____
_____
_____

Name: _____

Time 1: _____ Time 2: _____

The Championship Match

The sun blazed overhead as the crowd gathered for the championship soccer match. Among the players was Alex, a determined young athlete with dreams of victory. The referee's whistle pierced the air, signaling the start of the game. Alex's heart pounded with anticipation as they sprinted across the field. The ball weaved between players, and the cheers of the crowd filled the stadium. Alex showcased agility and skill, dribbling past opponents with precision. Teammates worked in harmony, passing with accuracy and executing strategic plays. The game was intense, both sides fighting for glory. With minutes remaining, the score was tied. Determined, Alex pushed forward, fueled by the desire to win. In a swift moment, they struck the ball, sending it soaring into the net. The crowd erupted in thunderous applause as Alex's team celebrated the winning goal. Victory was sweet, but the journey and the bonds forged were equally cherished. As the trophy was lifted high, Alex realized the true power of teamwork, determination, and the joy that comes from giving your all on the field.

Name: _____

Time 1: _____ Time 2: _____

Comprehension

Characters:

_____
_____
_____

Setting

_____
_____
_____

Summary

_____
_____
_____
_____
_____
_____

Name: _____

Time 1: _____ Time 2: _____

The Secret of the Moonlight

In a mysterious forest, a young boy named Jack stumbled upon a hidden cave. Little did he know, it was the dwelling place of werewolves. On a moonlit night, Jack witnessed a transformation like no other. The werewolves, under the full moon's enchantment, turned into powerful creatures. Curiosity sparked within Jack as he embarked on a journey to learn more. With each encounter, he discovered the werewolves' struggle to control their wild instincts. Jack befriended Liam, a young werewolf with a kind heart. Together, they searched for a way to break the moon's spell and grant the werewolves peace. Their quest led them to an ancient artifact guarded by a formidable creature. With courage and cleverness, they outwitted the guardian and obtained the artifact. In a solemn ritual, the artifact's power was harnessed, allowing the werewolves to regain control during full moons. Jack and Liam's bond grew stronger, united by their shared triumph. Word of their achievement spread, and humans and werewolves learned to coexist, fostering a newfound understanding. The forest became a sanctuary where humans and werewolves thrived together, celebrating the harmony they had achieved.

Name: _____

Time 1: _____ Time 2: _____

Comprehension

Characters:
_____
_____
_____

Setting
_____
_____
_____

Summary
_____
_____
_____
_____
_____
_____
_____

Name: _____

Time 1: _____ Time 2: _____

The Epic Battle: The Splash vs. The Chained

In a bustling city, a superhero named The Splash protected the innocent with their extraordinary water-based powers. But a formidable foe, known as The Chained, sought to bring chaos and destruction. The Chained unleashed their dark powers, ensnaring the city in chains of despair. Buildings trembled as citizens cried out for help. Determined to save the day, The Splash sprang into action. Their hands summoned torrents of water, washing away the chains and restoring hope. The Splash and The Chained clashed, their powers colliding in a dazzling display of light and darkness. The battle raged on, shaking the very foundations of the city. With unwavering resolve, The Splash unleashed a powerful tidal wave, washing away The Chained's malevolence. The villain's chains shattered, leaving them powerless. The citizens rejoiced as The Splash emerged victorious, their heroism celebrated throughout the city. The Chained, now defeated, was taken into custody, ensuring peace for all. As The Splash stood tall, they vowed to protect the city and its people from any threat. Their presence inspired others to stand up against evil and make a difference.

Name: _____

Time 1: _____ Time 2: _____

Comprehension

Characters:

_____
_____
_____

Setting

_____
_____
_____

Summary

_____
_____
_____
_____
_____
_____
_____

Name: _____

Time 1: _____ Time 2: _____

The Time Traveler's Adventure

In a small attic, Emma discovered a dusty old pocket watch. Little did she know, it held the power of time travel. Curiosity sparked within Emma as she turned the watch's golden hands. Suddenly, she found herself transported to a different era. Amidst ancient ruins, she encountered a wise old sage who revealed the watch's secret. Emma could explore different time periods, witnessing history firsthand. With a heart full of excitement, Emma embarked on incredible journeys. She met famous figures, explored distant lands, and witnessed pivotal moments in time. However, she soon realized that altering the past could have dire consequences. Emma learned the importance of preserving history and making wise choices.

With newfound knowledge, Emma returned to her time, cherishing the experiences and sharing her stories with others. The attic became a portal to endless possibilities, reminding Emma and others that the past holds lessons and the present is a canvas for their own adventures.

Name: _____

Time 1: _____ Time 2: _____

Comprehension

Characters:

_____

_____

_____

Setting

_____

_____

_____

Summary

_____

_____

_____

_____

_____

_____

Name: _____

Time 1: _____ Time 2: _____

The Unlikely Friendship: Shark and Whale

In the vast ocean, a fierce shark named Finn swam with unmatched speed and agility. One day, he encountered a gentle giant—the magnificent whale named Willow.

At first, fear and uncertainty filled their hearts, but curiosity prevailed. They set aside their differences and embarked on an extraordinary journey together.

Finn marveled at Willow's graceful movements, and Willow admired Finn's strength and determination. They soon discovered they had more in common than they initially thought. As their friendship deepened, Finn and Willow learned about the ocean's delicate balance and the threats it faced. They joined forces to protect their home from pollution and overfishing. Their united voices resonated throughout the ocean, inspiring other sea creatures to stand up for their rights. Together, they created a sanctuary where marine life could thrive. Finn and Willow became ambassadors for friendship and conservation. Their tale spread across the seas, reminding all creatures of the power of unity and the importance of preserving our oceans.

Name: _____

Time 1: _____ Time 2: _____

Comprehension

Characters:

_____
_____
_____

Setting

_____
_____
_____

Summary

_____
_____
_____
_____
_____
_____
_____

Name: _____

Time 1: _____ Time 2: _____

The Ninja's Quest

In the shadows of ancient Japan, a young ninja named Hiro honed his skills in the art of stealth and combat. Guided by his master, he prepared for a perilous mission.
Hiro's journey led him to a remote village, tormented by an evil warlord. With each step, he faced traps and foes, using his agility and wit to overcome them. Disguised as a humble traveler, Hiro infiltrated the warlord's stronghold. He discovered a secret plot to enslave the village, threatening innocent lives. With swift precision, Hiro fought against the warlord's henchmen, using his ninja weapons and ancient techniques. The battle was fierce, but Hiro's determination never wavered. In a final showdown, Hiro faced the warlord himself. Their clash echoed through the halls, each strike propelled by the desire to protect the innocent. With a well-aimed blow, Hiro defeated the warlord, liberating the village from tyranny. Grateful villagers celebrated their newfound freedom, their fears replaced with hope. Hiro's bravery and skills earned him the title of legendary ninja. His story inspired others to stand against injustice, embracing the principles of honor and courage.

Name: _____
Time 1: _____ Time 2: _____

Comprehension

Characters:
_____
_____
_____

Setting
_____
_____
_____

Summary
_____
_____
_____
_____
_____
_____
_____

Name: _____

Time 1: _____ Time 2: _____

The Enchanting Prom Night

Excitement filled the air as the school buzzed with preparations for the long-awaited prom. Emily, a shy but determined student, eagerly anticipated the magical evening. As the night unfolded, the gymnasium transformed into a dazzling wonderland. Twinkling lights adorned the walls, and a DJ played rhythmic beats. Dressed in their finest attire, students flooded the dance floor. Laughter and music filled the room as they danced, creating unforgettable memories. Emily mustered the courage to ask her crush, Jake, for a dance. Nervously, she approached him, heart pounding. To her delight, he accepted with a smile. They swayed to the music, the world fading away as they locked eyes. In that moment, everything felt perfect. Friendships were celebrated, and memories were etched into hearts. The crowning of prom king and queen added to the joy and anticipation of the night. As the evening drew to a close, students left with beaming smiles, cherishing the bonds forged on this special night. Prom became a cherished memory, reminding them of their resilience and the power of shared experiences.

Name: _____

Time 1: _____ Time 2: _____

Comprehension

Characters:

_____
_____
_____

Setting

_____
_____
_____

Summary

_____
_____
_____
_____
_____
_____

Name: _____

Time 1: _____ Time 2: _____

The Thrilling Hockey Game

The crowd roared with excitement as the hockey teams took the ice. Sarah, a passionate young player, felt a surge of adrenaline as she stepped onto the rink. The referee dropped the puck, and the game began. Sarah swiftly maneuvered, showcasing her skills with every stride. The puck flew across the ice as teammates passed with precision. The opponents fought back fiercely, creating a thrilling contest.

Sarah's determination never wavered. She expertly dodged opponents and shot the puck, sending it soaring towards the net. Cheers erupted as Sarah's shot found its mark, scoring a goal for her team. The stadium reverberated with the collective joy of victory. The game intensified as the clock ticked down. Both teams battled relentlessly, displaying their love for the sport. With seconds remaining, the score was tied. In a heart-stopping moment, Sarah seized an opportunity and scored the winning goal, sealing the victory. The crowd erupted in applause, celebrating the team's triumph. Sarah's teammates lifted her high, basking in the glory of a hard-fought win. The game taught Sarah the value of teamwork, perseverance, and the exhilaration of chasing her dreams on the ice.

Name: _____

Time 1: _____ Time 2: _____

Comprehension

Characters:

_____

_____

_____

Setting

_____

_____

_____

Summary

_____

_____

_____

_____

_____

_____

_____

Name: _____

Time 1: _____ Time 2: _____

The Memorable Field Trip

Excitement filled the air as the school bus pulled away, embarking on a thrilling field trip. The destination? The Natural History Museum. The students marveled at the towering dinosaur skeletons and ancient artifacts. The exhibits came alive with stories of the past, capturing their imagination. Their tour guide, Ms. Adams, led them through galleries, sharing fascinating facts and engaging anecdotes. Students scribbled notes and took in the wonders around them. One exhibit, in particular, caught their attention—an interactive fossil dig. With brushes in hand, they unearthed replicas of dinosaur bones, feeling like real paleontologists. Next, they explored the planetarium, where a breathtaking show transported them across the galaxy. Twinkling stars and celestial wonders filled their eyes. Lunchtime brought laughter and camaraderie as classmates shared sandwiches and stories. The day continued with a walk through a simulated rainforest, complete with exotic plants and animal sounds. As the field trip came to an end, students boarded the bus, filled with newfound knowledge and cherished memories.

Name: _____
Time 1: _____ Time 2: _____

Comprehension

Characters:
_____
_____
_____

Setting
_____
_____
_____

Summary
_____
_____
_____
_____
_____
_____
_____

Name: _____

Time 1: _____ Time 2: _____

The Lion and the Cheetah's Friendship

In the vast savannah, a proud lion named Leo ruled over his territory. One day, he crossed paths with a swift cheetah named Chloe. Initially cautious, Leo and Chloe soon realized they shared a common love for their homeland. They set aside their differences and forged an unlikely friendship. Leo's strength and wisdom complemented Chloe's speed and agility. Together, they embarked on daring adventures, exploring the wonders of the wild. With Leo's guidance, Chloe learned valuable lessons about survival and leadership. In return, Chloe's lightning-fast reflexes amazed Leo, inspiring him to embrace agility. Their friendship grew stronger as they protected their fellow animals from threats. They patrolled the savannah, ensuring peace and harmony among the creatures. One day, they faced a raging wildfire that threatened their home. Leo and Chloe rallied the animals, leading them to safety and extinguishing the flames together. Their bravery and teamwork became legendary, earning the respect of all who witnessed their actions. The lion and the cheetah united the savannah's inhabitants, creating a strong bond among different species.

Name: _____

Time 1: _____ Time 2: _____

Comprehension

Characters:
_____
_____
_____

Setting
_____
_____
_____

Summary
_____
_____
_____
_____
_____
_____

Name: _____

Time 1: _____ Time 2: _____

The Creative Journey: TV Show Writer

Meet Lily, an imaginative sixth grader with a passion for storytelling. Her dream? To become a TV show writer. With a notebook and pen in hand, she embarked on a creative journey. Lily weaved captivating tales, crafting characters and plot twists that mesmerized her friends. She drew inspiration from everyday life and her vivid imagination. One day, Lily's talent caught the attention of a famous TV producer. He invited her to join a team of writers for a popular show. Excitement filled Lily's heart as she sat in the writers' room, brainstorming ideas and bringing stories to life. She learned the art of collaboration and the power of revision. Through late nights and countless rewrites, Lily honed her skills. Her words danced on the screen, captivating audiences and leaving them craving more. Lily's dream had come true. She had become a TV show writer, making an impact with her stories.

Her journey taught her the value of perseverance, teamwork, and the importance of believing in oneself. Lily's imagination continued to soar, as she inspired others to follow their creative dreams.

Name: _____

Time 1: _____ Time 2: _____

Comprehension

Characters:
_____
_____
_____

Setting
_____
_____
_____

Summary
_____
_____
_____
_____
_____
_____
_____

Name: _____

Time 1: _____ Time 2: _____

The Melodic Journey: TV Musician

Meet Max, a talented sixth grader with a passion for music. His dream? To become a TV musician. With his guitar in hand and a melody in his heart, he embarked on a melodic journey. Max strummed his guitar and composed catchy tunes that resonated with his friends. His music filled the air with joy and rhythm. One day, Max's talent caught the attention of a renowned TV producer. He invited Max to perform his music on a popular show. Nervously, Max took the stage, surrounded by bright lights and cameras. He played his guitar with passion, and his voice soared with every note. The audience was captivated by Max's talent, and his music touched their hearts. They clapped and sang along, embracing the magic of his melodies. Max's dream had come true. He had become a TV musician, sharing his gift with the world. His journey taught him the value of practice, perseverance, and the power of music to bring people together. Max's melodies continued to inspire others, encouraging them to pursue their own musical dreams.

Name: _____
Time 1: _____ Time 2: _____

Comprehension

Characters:
_____
_____
_____

Setting
_____
_____
_____

Summary
_____
_____
_____
_____
_____
_____
_____

Name: _____

Time 1: _____ Time 2: _____

The Brave Knight and the Evil Crow

In the kingdom of Arindale, a brave knight named Sir William stood tall. One day, an evil crow named Malachi cast a dark shadow over the land. Malachi wreaked havoc, stealing treasures and spreading fear. Sir William, armed with his sword and shield, vowed to defeat the wicked creature. Through treacherous forests and perilous mountains, the knight pursued the crow. Their epic battle unfolded in the castle's crumbling courtyard.

Sir William fought valiantly, parrying the crow's sharp beak and claws. With a final swing, he vanquished Malachi, freeing the kingdom from his reign of terror. The people rejoiced, honoring Sir William as a hero. The kingdom flourished once more, basking in the light of peace and justice. Sir William's courage and determination inspired others, reminding them of the power of good over evil. The legend of the knight and the evil crow echoed throughout the land, reminding all that bravery and valor can conquer any challenge.

Name: _____
Time 1: _____ Time 2: _____

Comprehension

Characters:
_____
_____
_____

Setting
_____
_____
_____

Summary
_____
_____
_____
_____
_____
_____

Name: _____

Time 1: _____ Time 2: _____

The Case of the Missing Pizza

In the quiet town of Ridgemont, a hilarious mystery unfolded. The beloved pizza truck, Pizza Paradise, vanished overnight, leaving residents hungry for answers. Enter Jack and Emily, a dynamic duo with a knack for solving silly mysteries. Armed with magnifying glasses and detective hats, they embarked on their funniest case yet. Clues led them to a trail of pizza crumbs and suspicious laughter. They followed the scent of melted cheese to the local park, where they discovered a mischievous squirrel hoarding slices. The furry culprit, named Cheesy, had developed a taste for pizza. Jack and Emily, with laughter in their hearts, confronted Cheesy and struck a deal: pizza in exchange for returning the stolen truck. The town rejoiced as Pizza Paradise rolled back into Ridgemont, and Cheesy became the park's honorary pizza inspector. Jack and Emily became the heroes of the day, solving the hilarious mystery that had left everyone puzzled. Ridgemont learned that sometimes even the silliest mysteries can bring unexpected smiles and full stomachs.

Name: _____
Time 1: _____ Time 2: _____

Comprehension

Characters:
_____
_____
_____

Setting
_____
_____
_____

Summary
_____
_____
_____
_____
_____
_____

Name: _____

Time 1: _____ Time 2: _____

The Extraordinary Expedition: Journey to an Alien Planet

Imagine a world beyond our wildest dreams. In the year 3021, a group of intrepid explorers embarked on an extraordinary expedition to an alien planet. Equipped with state-of-the-art spacecraft, they soared through the vastness of space, brimming with excitement and curiosity. As they landed on the alien planet's surface, they marveled at the vibrant colors and peculiar flora. Strange creatures scurried about, their curiosity matching the explorers'. Communication was a challenge, but a friendly alien named Zara emerged. With gestures and laughter, they formed a bond, exploring the wonders of the alien planet together. The explorers discovered magnificent landscapes, shimmering lakes, and breathtaking vistas. They marveled at the peculiarities of this new world, capturing every moment with awe. But as their time on the alien planet drew to a close, a sense of longing settled in their hearts. They said heartfelt goodbyes to Zara, promising to return someday. Back on their spaceship, the explorers reflected on their incredible journey. The alien planet had taught them to embrace the unknown, cherish diversity, and appreciate the beauty of discovery.

Name: _____
Time 1: _____ Time 2: _____

Comprehension

Characters:
_____
_____
_____

Setting
_____
_____
_____

Summary
_____
_____
_____
_____
_____
_____
_____

Name: _____

Time 1: _____ Time 2: _____

The Epic Quest: Journey to the Monkey King

In a mystical land, a brave group of adventurers set out on an epic quest to seek the legendary Monkey King. Their mission? To obtain his wisdom and guidance. Through treacherous jungles and towering mountains, they overcame obstacles and faced fantastical creatures. Their determination never wavered. Finally, they arrived at the sacred Monkey King's realm. With respect and awe, they presented their request for his wisdom. The Monkey King, known for his mischievous spirit, challenged them to a series of mind-bending riddles and physical tests. Laughter filled the air as they attempted each trial. Impressed by their courage and wit, the Monkey King bestowed his wisdom upon them. He shared ancient tales and valuable life lessons that would guide them on their own journeys. With gratitude in their hearts, the adventurers bid farewell to the Monkey King. They returned to their land, forever changed by their encounter. Armed with newfound knowledge, they faced life's challenges with resilience and a playful spirit, inspired by the Monkey King's indomitable nature.

Name: _____

Time 1: _____ Time 2: _____

Comprehension

Characters:
_____
_____
_____

Setting
_____
_____
_____

Summary
_____
_____
_____
_____
_____
_____
_____

Name: _____

Time 1: _____ Time 2: _____

The Brave Knight and the Evil Crow

Whiskers, the mischievous but talented cat, had a unique passion for cooking. Armed with a whisk and a chef's hat, he embarked on his culinary adventures.

In his cozy kitchen, Whiskers concocted delectable dishes, experimenting with flavors and textures. His whisk swirled through the air, adding a touch of magic to each creation. Word of Whiskers' culinary talents spread like wildfire, reaching the ears of renowned chefs. They invited him to a prestigious cooking competition. With nerves and excitement, Whiskers entered the grand kitchen, ready to prove his skills. He whipped up dishes with finesse, captivating the judges' taste buds. The competition was fierce, but Whiskers' unique flair and dedication set him apart. He won the hearts of the judges, earning the title of the "Cat Chef." Whiskers' fame soared as he opened his own bistro, serving mouthwatering meals to feline food enthusiasts. His purrs of delight echoed through the restaurant. From that day forward, Whiskers' name became synonymous with culinary excellence. His whisk remained his trusted tool as he continued to inspire aspiring chefs around the world.

Name: _____

Time 1: _____ Time 2: _____

Comprehension

Characters:
_____
_____
_____

Setting
_____
_____
_____

Summary
_____
_____
_____
_____
_____
_____
_____

Name: _____

Time 1: _____ Time 2: _____

The Brave Knight and the Evil Crow

In Metropolis, an epic track meet unfolded, bringing together the mightiest superheroes from all corners of the universe. The crowd buzzed with excitement as Superman, The Flash, and Wonder Woman stood at the starting line. The signal sounded, and they sprinted forward with unparalleled speed. Superman soared through the air, leaving spectators in awe. The Flash blazed across the track like lightning. Wonder Woman's grace and strength were unmatched. Cheers erupted as they raced towards the finish line. Though their powers were extraordinary, their sportsmanship was even more admirable. They pushed each other to their limits, celebrating one another's achievements. As the dust settled, they exchanged smiles and handshakes, united by their love for justice and competition. The track meet showcased the true spirit of heroism, reminding everyone that we all have the potential to be superheroes in our own way. Metropolis cheered their heroes, grateful for their inspiration. The legacy of this incredible track meet would live on, encouraging others to reach for the stars.

Name: _____

Time 1: _____ Time 2: _____

Comprehension

Characters:

_____

_____

_____

Setting

_____

_____

_____

Summary

_____

_____

_____

_____

_____

_____

_____

Name: _____

Time 1: _____ Time 2: _____

The Environmental Heroes

Ava, Jacob, Olivia, and Noah came together as environmental activists, driven by their deep concern for the planet. With unwavering determination, they formed a group of environmental heroes, committed to making a difference. They organized tree-planting initiatives, rolling up their sleeves to restore green spaces and combat deforestation. They tirelessly advocated for renewable energy sources, raising awareness about the importance of transitioning to a sustainable future. Their passionate efforts didn't go unnoticed as they inspired their community to take action. Through educational campaigns, they encouraged others to adopt eco-friendly practices, reduce waste, and conserve resources. The collective actions of these young environmental heroes sparked a positive change, cultivating a sense of responsibility and a shared commitment to protect the planet for generations to come.

Made in the USA
Columbia, SC
23 January 2025